THE YEAR
AT MAPLE HILL FARM

WINTER

SPRING

SUMMER

AUTUMN

Alice and Martin Provensen

A JONATHAN CAPE BOOK

ATHENEUM 1978 NEW YORK

For Dinah

Library of Congress Cataloging in Publication Data

Provensen, Alice.
   The year at Maple Hill Farm.

   "A Jonathan Cape Book
   SUMMARY: Describes the seasonal changes on a farm
and surrounding countryside throughout the year.
   [1. Farm life—Fiction. 2. Seasons—Fiction]
I. Provensen, Martin, joint author. II Title.
PZ7.P9457Yl 1978   [E]   77-18518
Trade Edition ISBN 0-689-30642-3
Spartan Edition ISBN 0-689-20494-9

Copyright © 1978 by Alice and Martin Provensen
All rights reserved
Printed in the United States of America by
A. Hoen & Co., Baltimore, Maryland
Bound by The Book Press, Inc.,
Brattleboro, Vermont
First Edition

THE YEAR

This is a book about farm animals,
And what happens during one year on a farm.

The year is divided into twelve months,
The months are divided into weeks,
The weeks into days,
The days into minutes,
And on a farm something is happening every minute.

Animals don't know there is such a thing as a year,
But they do know about seasons.
Animals know when the cold will come,
And they grow heavy overcoats.
They know when it is summer,
And they shed them.
When it is hot, they look for shade,
And in winter, they look for shelter.

People have names for what they call the months of the year.
We could start with any month as far as the animals are concerned,
But it is usual to begin with January.

January is a winter month. The ground is covered with snow.

Cows stay in the barnyard when the ground is frozen. So do the chickens,
but not many eggs are laid in January. The days are too short and dark.
The horses don't mind the cold. Neither do the sheep with their heavy winter coats.

It is a cold, grey time of year and night falls early.

All the farm animals stay close to the barn where they are fed.
There is hay and grain to eat. Even the wild deer come nearer the farm,
hoping to find a little salt or a windfall apple under the snow.

The children are having a skating party. When they are cold, they sit by the fire and toast their toes and noses. The geese play in the icy water all winter. You'd think their bare feet would freeze but they never do.

all but a marshy place where the spring water feeds the pond.

The noisy rooks are having a circus. They toss and tumble on the trapezes of bare branches. Rooks like winter. Under the ice, in a tunnel in the frozen ground, the water rat is napping. He won't be up until spring.

March is a windy month. It is still cold outside but you can tell spring is coming. There are signs of spring in the barn.

The pony has given birth to a foal.
She loves him and looks after him.

The milk cow has a new calf.
She loves him and gives him her milk.

The good grey barn cat has her
litter of kittens in the hay rack.
The mother ewe has two new lambs.

The nanny goat has a new kid, too.
All the animal mothers are proud
and protective and full of love.

March is windy and rainy, but when the sun does shine, it shines more brightly and the days are longer. There are signs of spring everywhere.

The robins are back and are busy building their nests.

A wild duck is in the marsh marigolds.

The rooster wakes everyone earlier in the morning.

The geese are cranky. They must have laid an egg.

The meadow mice are out looking around.

The mad March hare is hurrying in all directions.

The ice on the pond has melted and there are pussy willows. The horses have found a little grass under the last patches of snow. They lie down in the pale sunshine. You don't see that often if the ground is frozen.

April is a spring month. You can tell that spring is here by all the eggs.

The good old brown hen has been busy sitting on eggs for twenty-one days. Now her baby chicks are hatching. It must be hard to pick your way out of an egg, but the chicks are pretty and fluffy in no time.

Eggs in the barn, in the fields, in the trees, under the eaves, everywhere.

The robins are already hatching
eggs in their business-like way.

This silly goose has laid an egg in
the middle of nowhere. She must be crazy.

This big bird is laying her egg in a
little bird's nest. She must be cuckoo.

This little bird is feeding her babies.
She must wonder why one baby is so big.

Here is a basket of coloured eggs
among the flowers.
No one has found it yet.

Dogs steal eggs when they can find
them and carry them away.
Perhaps dogs make nests, too.

May days are warm. The animals are uncomfortable with their heavy coats.

Everyone gets a haircut one way or another. The woolly sheep are shorn.

The black sheep-dog is shorn at the same time — not a very fancy clip.
She will scarcely be recognizable without her long curls, but they will
grow back in time for winter and she will look herself again.

They will all be cooler without them. Even the chickens moult.

The rooster won't be himself until he can parade his fine tail feathers again.

Even though it's cool and comfortable, it must be embarrassing
to lose all your clothes all at once. Cats don't need clipping.
They shed their coats on other people's clothes and furniture.

June is the first month of summer. The farm pond is overflowing.

Horses eat grass. Geese eat grass. Cows and sheep and goats eat grass. Chickens eat grass, too, but that's not the reason the chickens are out in the pasture—they are chasing insects. The horses stir up insects with their big feet. Chickens love insects.

The pasture is green. All the animals enjoy the new green grass.

The mother duck is out on the pond. She is teaching her ducklings to swim. Someone else is out today, too. The good grey cat is teaching her kittens to hunt. That bird is safe on his branch, but those squirrels had better watch out—cats don't eat grass or insects.

In June there are enough insects to go around.
The fields are hopping with insects—grasshoppers and leaf-hoppers and tree-hoppers.

There are plenty of flies around in June—
Dragon-flies and mayflies and blue flies and butterflies.

In June there are enough horse-flies to go around and around.

In summer the fields are full of flowers.
Goats and sheep like flowers. Bees like flowers. Everyone likes flowers.

The flowers are buzzing with bees—bumble-bees and honey-bees and busy bees.
Flowers like bees. They need them.

In summer the grass is hopping with fleas. No one likes fleas. They bite.

There are so many sounds to listen to.
Frogs croak. Crickets chirp. An owl is hooting to another owl.
The old people on the porch are chatting in low voices about old times.
A cow lows now and then.

if the moon is full and shining and the summer stars are out.

You can hear the steady clank of the conveyor carrying the sweet-scented hay to the loft in the barn. You can hear the quiet laughter of the men as they work.
You can hear a mother goose hissing softly, warning strangers from her nest in the shed.
Sometimes, if everything is silent for a moment, you can hear the horses eating grass.

August is the last summer month. The sky is blue. The sun shines.

The sun shines and shines.
The cows doze away the noonday.

The sheep graze and graze all day.
The lambs are growing by the minute.

The flowers are growing, too. Flowers
need hours of attention in August heat.

The vegetables need attention, too. Someone
is stealing lettuce. What good is a watchdog?

Late summer is a drowsy time of year. The days are hot and lazy.

Almost asleep in a puddle of dust, a dog will still wag his tail as you walk by.

The geese are quieter in August. All the noisy nesting is over for a while.

The pig has tipped over her pail. Now she has a cool mud puddle to sleep in.

You know it is hot when that old cat comes out for a breath of air.

Then, sometimes quite suddenly, a fresh wind blows
and the summer is over. The days are shorter. September is here.

Everyone begins to wake up after the heat of summer.
The evenings are pleasant in September and the horses are lively.

They are brought in from the field to be shod.
The horses aren't afraid of the blacksmith. They are used to him.
They don't mind having their shoes nailed on. It doesn't hurt.

Now the days are cooler and a sense of change is in the air.
September is the first month of autumn.

Autumn is a fine time for riding, even if it's raining. Most animals
don't mind raindrops but the big bay horse is ticklish and doesn't
want to leave his stall. Animals can be very temperamental.

Animals, just as people do, sometimes have to take medicine.
They have to take worm medicine and they don't like it much.

Some dogs will eat their pill
if it's wrapped up in cheese
and they can't smell it.

Some dogs don't care
what they eat, no
matter how it smells.

Geese never need worming.
They even eat worms.
They are lucky.

Sheep will stand quietly to take
their medicine — if you get a good
grip on them and hold their noses.

Most cats will eat their medicine mixed up in their
dinner, but there is always a scratchy one who must
be wrapped in a towel to have her pill pushed down.

While most animals will take their medicine without too much of
an argument, there are some who won't.

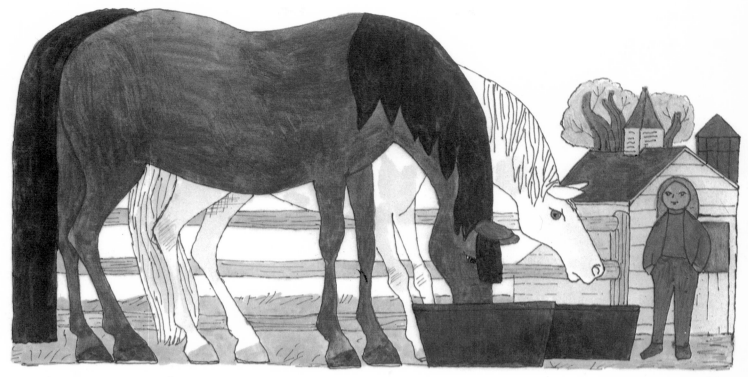

Some horses never make
a fuss about pills.
They don't taste so bad.

Some horses are suspicious
if pills are put in their grain.
It's not the taste, it's the smell that worries them.

It's not easy to hold a temperamental horse's nose—and you can't wrap up a horse in
a towel. The vet has to be called, and he needs a helper to get the medicine down.
Frightening as it is, it will all be forgotten in a minute. Animals don't hold grudges.

October is a splendid month. The harvest is in.
An early frost did away with all the insects.

The hay is in the barn. The corn is in the crib. There's not much left to eat in the fields and the animals stay closer to the barnyard. The chickens go to roost earlier and not so many eggs are laid.

October days are dry and bright but·still the wild birds are restless and begin to flock together.

The children gather pumpkins. The squirrels are gathering nuts, filling their own storehouses with food. Soon the leaves will all be gone. At any moment the migrant birds will rise and start their journey south.

November! There is a frost nearly every night now. The air smells of snow and winter. The first thin ice is forming on the farm pond.

The woods around the farm echo the huntsman's horn. The hunting hounds bay.

In November, before winter comes finally, a few of the animals leave the farm. Some are sold, the finest are borrowed by the neighbours for breeding.

The north wind blows. The bare branches rattle. The forest is far from quiet in November before the winter settles in.

The wild geese honk as they pass by. The saw and the woodsmen are noisy too.

A few ganders are sent along as gifts. Everyone likes ganders.
You can't have too many ganders—except in the barn through the winter.

Now is the time to be in the barn. There is hay and grain to eat.
There are places to play or hide or dream. There are warm straw beds.

with snow. The days are dark and cold and night falls early.

December is the last month of the year. Now is the time to catch up on sleep. Everyone goes to bed earlier in wintertime.

An old barn owl is the only one awake
to greet the January of another year.

No, here are the deer, come silently to the barnyard
for a bit of salt and a little left-over hay.

And the quiet fox is making certain
the chickens are safe in bed this New Year's Eve.